50
QUESTIONS
for
THINKING
CHRISTIANS

STEVE BASKA

50 Questions for Thinking Christians

978-0-9989974-1-4 (Paperback)
978-0-9989974-0-7 (eBook)

Published in the United States
by Jayhawk Mountain Press, Castle Pines, Colorado

Acknowledgements

Thanks to Rev. Adam Hamilton, senior pastor of Church of the Resurrection, a Methodist church in Leawood, KS; to my wife Vickie, my brother Scott, and my pastors at St. Andrew United Methodist Church in south Denver, especially Senior Pastor Mark Feldmeir.

Contents

Introduction

This small book aims to spur thought and discussion about living the Christian faith, but it can also be applied to other faiths. The term "thinking Christians" in the title seems a popular term at this time, and indicates a desire to think deeply about issues rather than simply accepting what we have been told or taught in the past without questioning. The commentaries in this book mention the "conservative" and "liberal" Christian views on these theological topics because, in this era, people's views are often identified as in either of those two camps. I find it helpful to try to understand both those sides of the issues, and hope the reader does also. This book is also a compilation of my thoughts and readings on the basics elements of the Christian faith. Where information is taken from a particular source, it is cited. I hope this book can be used as a resource for individuals, families, small group discussions and sermons.

SECTION ONE:
Your Personal Faith

QUESTION

1

How would you describe your religious beliefs in one minute?

Comments: If a stranger or a friend asked you what you think of God and religion, what would you say? Could you summarize your beliefs? It helps to be short, clear and to the point, but what would you say and include? Many people have never thought to summarize and clarify their beliefs in a way to simply explain them. One possible answer is like this: "I am a traditional conservative Christian. I believe there is a personal God who created the universe, and an afterlife in Heaven, and that Jesus was God who came to earth in a man's body, and he was physically resurrected, and the Bible is a true and reliable history of God's interaction with man."

These areas cover several of the major areas of faith discussions, and communicate your beliefs quickly to someone. Or you may wish to say your beliefs are not traditional as a Christian. You may say "I am a more moderate or liberal Christian. I believe in God and an afterlife, but not in Jesus as God, and not that the Bible is to be taken literally or reliably in many points. I believe the Bible has errors and was written by men trying to hear and understand God."

These two types of answers also point out that faith beliefs and Christians are often categorized quickly today as either conservative or liberal. Many people will place you on that scale according to your answers because it is easy to categorize people that way. But don't be deterred from answering what you truly believe, and then let the discussion go from there. You also may wish to say your faith is of high importance to you and your practices include prayer, Bible study, church attendance and service to the poor and needy. This will give a stranger an idea of what active areas your faith includes, and may spur a lively conversation.

QUESTION 2

How did you decide on your religious beliefs?

Comments: This question tries to uncover how your beliefs were formed and accepted. Did you accept them from your earliest years due to family and peer influences? Or perhaps the opposite: Did you reject family and peer beliefs as a youthful rebellion? If you had grown up in a Muslim family, do you think you would be Muslim?

As a thinking Christian, coming to your own decisions by honest evaluations is hopefully important to you. Do you weigh both sides of an issue, look for evidence, consider the opinion of experts? Can you also make a leap of faith based on intuition if you feel it is correct? Also, you may ask what role have emotions played in your decisions? Do you believe in God simply because it is comforting to have that support in hard times and you enjoy holding a rosy vision of an afterlife?

In my Methodist denomination, we are encouraged to form beliefs based on four things: Scripture, reason, tradition and experience. We start with Bible scripture, but then to understand the passages more fully, we also apply our own reason, and the thoughts and traditions of 2,000 years of the church, and our own experience with the issues.

This is called the Wesley Quadrilateral, meaning four elements that were suggested by the Methodist founder John Wesley. This can be a good model for evaluating all types of beliefs, including social, personal and political. For example, do you hold the same political views as your family and friends? If so, why is that?

QUESTION 3

Have you ever changed your views on an important aspect of faith?

Comments: Many people come to Christian faith in their youth, form their beliefs then, and then never change. Some view that as a good thing: God does not change and neither should we, they say. Others say that we grow in wisdom and understanding as we age, so our views should naturally change. Is it wise to keep all the same views you had as a teenager?

An important underlying question is: Are you willing to change if you think it is right, or do you see change as a betrayal of your faith and something that will cause criticism from your family and peers? Often when politicians change their views on gun control, abortion or homosexuality, they are termed "flip floppers" and are attacked as unreliable, even pandering to get votes. But if their change is authentic and heartfelt, and as when real information and situations change, should we not allow people to change? For example, there was a time when people thought the Earth was flat. But science eventually showed that the Earth is round and people came to accept that change in their views.

As Christians we rejoice when someone changes from non-belief to accepting and following Christ, but we often criticize those who change within the Christian circle. There are at least three ways to look at change: People can be too resistant to change, or can be willing to change when convinced adequately of the need, or they can be too eager to change by jumping on any new popular idea. Where would you say you are on this scale? Some societies today are changing on social issues, including the acceptance of gay marriage, for example. Could you be open to changing your mind on this or other issues?

"But grow in grace, and in the knowledge of our Lord and Savior Jesus Christ. To Him be glory both now and forever. Amen" (II PETER 3:18).

QUESTION 4

Are you progressing through the four stages of faith growth?

Comments: The Christian faith journey should be a growing from newness to spiritual maturity in all the practices of the faith. The journey is often compared to four stages of human life: baby, child, young adult, mature adult.

First is the newborn baby entering this new world and observing and hearing the language. Then the young child is learning the concepts of this new world, and the child often naturally accepts what his or her parents and peers believe. Thirdly, the child becomes a young adult with a growing knowledge and desire to think for himself or herself, so they begin to question and challenge and study more deeply. Finally, as a mature adult, the person uses his or her deep well of information and experience to form a mature belief system, which they use to shape their practices and then to share with younger people and all others in respectful ways.

Think back on when you became a new Christian. Whether you were a teenager, or a child, or an adult, you had some preconceptions, some basic knowledge of the Bible stories, and you observed those around you. You probably imitated their practices and soaked up their information. You found that the Bible was a mysterious book in many aspects, but you read it. As you grew in knowledge, you may have heard the saying "It's okay to have a 5th grade understanding of the Bible, as long as you are in the 5th grade." Sayings like that set the expectation that adults must keep growing. You began to learn about reading deeper, to use Bible commentaries to see what historians and others say about what the Bible's authors meant to say to their original audience, in their original language, not just what you in the current day think it clearly means.

Then as your life experience builds from years of reading, thinking, taking in all points of view, serving and being led by God, you finally feel differently than when you began: you have a well of knowledge to guide you and to share with others. You are not afraid of questions. You even have some answers and you have a comfort with not knowing the answers to everything. You can admit you may be wrong in some beliefs, and saying that does not make you feel diminished or ignorant. You have become a mature Christian.

When I was a child, I used to speak like a child, think like a child, reason like a child; when I became a man, I did away with childish things.
(1 CORINTHIANS 13:11)

SECTION TWO:
Your faith practices

What is on your list of faith practices and do you have a central notebook or other place to keep notes as you practice them?

Comments: Faith practices are all the things you do as you carry out your faith. This can include prayer, reading the Bible, reading other spiritual books, worshipping at a church or other place, music, service to others, sharing your faith beliefs, monetary support of God's work, showing symbols of your faith, mentoring others, working for social change, and the daily loving acts and attitudes toward people. This is just one example of a collection of practices. You may wish to add more of your own, such as meditation, journaling and many more that you do regularly or occasionally.

And in doing these, many people find it helpful to have one central notebook where you can keep notes in each category, such as a prayer list (of people to pray for), notes and questions about your Bible reading, sermon notes and so on. You may like one fat notebook, or several small notebooks (each dedicated to one practice), or perhaps you have gone paperless and keep notes on your computer. This section of the book examines each of these spiritual practices and makes suggestions about them.

QUESTION 6
What does your prayer life consist of?

Comments: Prayer is a very odd form of communication to us as humans. We are talking to an unseen person who lives in another dimension and who does not reply in standard human ways. It is so strange that many non-religious people think it is crazy, and probably many Christians pray only rarely. But just because it is unusual does not mean it is wrong or that God does not hear us. Prayer is speaking to a non-human, to a spirit, so a different method of communication and understanding is to be expected. Is it such a leap to believe a powerful creator, who is so far advanced beyond us can hear our words, even our thoughts? There was a time when people thought it was probably impossible to send words across a wire or even wirelessly, but we do that every day.

So, where, when and how do you pray? Muslims are directed to pray five times a day. Christians have no such requirement, except that we are to pray often. An easy way to pray is to do one long prayer each day and many short prayers. For the long prayer, use a written prayer list that you keep in your Bible or notebook. Keep a list of people to pray for, and pray down through your list, and tell those people that you are praying for them so they can feel your support.

Your prayer format can be by the popular acronym ACTS: Adoration (expressing love to God), Confession (admitting your failings, struggles), Thanksgiving (thanks for specific things), and Supplication (asking for help for other people and finally yourself). Pray for people in many categories: family, friends, local church, state leaders, national leaders, foreign leaders in crisis, for the broken world. If you need help to remember to pray, set a watch or alarm clock, or put a sticky note on your desk or bathroom mirror.

Then throughout the day, do short prayers: a thanks for food, a plea for help or wisdom before meeting someone. These are sometimes called "Breath Prayers," for being as short as one breath. Vary your prayers between written prayers and spontaneous. Keep copies of famous written prayers in your Bible, such as the Lord's Prayer. When you don't feel like making up your own prayer spontaneously, recite a written prayer or read a Psalm as a prayer.

Body position is another issue in prayer. You can sit with palms up, you can hold hands of other people, you can lift hands to the sky, you can kneel, you can lie flat on the ground. Vary your position, perhaps by doing something different each day. Mental focus is another consideration in prayer. Some people get frustrated because they let their thoughts drift off to other things in the middle of prayer. Keep concentration by following a list of things to pray about before you start into prayer.

Where to pray? Some people have a dedicated place to pray in their home. A corner with a special chair or prayer "kneeler". A Christian-focused movie called the "War Room" showed a lady with a closet that she converted to her prayer room, complete with written prayers and notes posted on the walls. When she went in her closet, she was serious about prayer. The physical place helped remind her of the importance of prayer. Do you have a "prayer chair" or other thing that can make prayer special for you?

Regarding expecting answers to prayer, some conservative Christians believe specific passages of the Bible can be relied on literally for an answer to whatever they pray for. Passages that say you can ask for anything and it will be given to you, or ask in Jesus name and it will be given to you, are taken as a clear promises by some. They name a desired outcome and name the passage and believe God is then somehow bound to fulfill their request. Liberal Christians often view prayer differently, believing that although we can ask for anything, God knows what is best and it is his will that should be fulfilled. Liberals believe you cannot pull out specific passages and take them individually without considering all related passages throughout the Bible.

What other aspects of prayer can you think that would help your prayer life?

Ask, and it will be given to you; seek and you will find; knock and it will be opened to you.
(MATTHEW 7:7)

QUESTION 7

How often, and how, do you read the Bible?

Comments: Do you read the Bible a little every day or week? Many Christians don't because they feel they have read it all before and so it fails to have an attractive newness to pull them in as a new novel or other book may for them. Or, many feel it is sufficient that they will hear a Biblical message in a Sunday sermon, so there's no need to continue reading it yourself. Regular reading is not their ingrained habit. But it is important to keep filling your mind with the stories and messages of the Bible. Make Bible reading easy and habitual. Set a time and place to read a few minutes every day. Put your Bible in an obvious place, such as on your bed or desk. Carry a pocket size New Testament with you to read in waiting times.

Where should you read? Start with Matthew, the first book of the New Testament, and go forward. Perhaps read one chapter a day. Reflect on the stories and the meaning. Then perhaps read the Psalms. Then read the Hebrew Bible, also called the Old Testament by Christians. Ask yourself: Is this book only a history of the Jewish people's practices in their time or is the advice meant to apply to us today? Conservatives and liberals can agree that many parts of the Old Testament are just historical recitations. For example, in Leviticus, the third book of the Hebrew Bible, there are many descriptions of rituals and laws about sacrifices and behavior that are commonly understood today as something meant only for the people of that time and place.

In other stories and commands, ask yourself if you think they are literally true, meaning did they really happened just as described, or are some stories meant to be symbolic, meaning they were made up to emphasize an important idea or point? For example, did Jesus really mean that we are to pluck out our eye if it causes us to sin? Many people say he was using exaggeration to make a point about how important is to guard against sin. Exaggeration, also called hyperbole, was a common practice in those days (and still today). Jesus did not really intend for everyone to pluck out their eyes. This is called putting a passage "in context," meaning how the author meant it to be understood in coordination with everything else he said. Look at commentary books or commentary notes in your Bible for extra insight. These are extra notes written by theologians to explain or interpret the meaning of Bible passages or themes.

We've likely all heard that there are "parables" in the Bible, meaning short stories that are made up (they did not happen in real life), but are meant to illustrate a moral point. Can you point to some of those? Some people say the story of Jonah living three days in the whale's belly then being spit up on shore is a fictional parable meant to show that you cannot run from God when he calls you to a task. Unfortunately, the Bible does not often identify which stories are fictional and which are real. A highly contentious question between conservatives and liberals remains whether God created man from dust in one moment, or through the process of evolution over millions of years. Is the dust story a fiction created so earlier people could understand the basic concept that God created man? Many conservatives do not think so, but liberals do. Liberal Christians see no problem in believing God used the evolutionary method.

Tell other people where you are reading in the Bible and ask what they think of it. Read by yourself or with a partner or in a small group. Take a short term or long term Bible study class. Over a lifetime you could become an expert about the Bible, even more than a recent seminary graduate. If a seminary student has four years of Bible classes, how much more could you learn little by little over 50 years of study and discussion. Would you agree with that? Why or why not?

QUESTION 8

How often do you read other spiritual books?

Comments: Are you one of those people who continually soak up the stories and knowledge from religious books other than the Bible? They offer tremendous insight and education to Christians. In the non-fiction category, there are biographies of how great Christians spent their lives and overcame challenges, there are books analyzing every book of the Bible, and there are books by pastors and scholars explaining every imaginable religious topic (grace, resurrection and so on). In the fiction category, there are imagined stories of God's people in all kinds of situations in days of old and today. These made-up stories entertain and educate on religious issues.

Get in the habit of reading widely many types of spiritual books and sharing lessons from them with others. Can you name a few of the most famous books in these categories? Among the top three on varied Christian best-seller lists have been: (1) The Purpose Driven Life: What on Earth Am I Here for? by Rick Warren; (2) : The Hiding Place, by Corrie Ten Boom; (3) Mere Christianity by C.S. Lewis. Classic top fiction books have included The Lion, the Witch, and the Wardrobe (Chronicles of Narnia, #1) by C.S. Lewis, and many books of Christian romance and adventure series.

Are you in habit of seeing what new Christian books are in the bookstores, or online or at the library, and then reading them? Why not? Are you not interested or feel it takes too much time or expense? Audio books can be listened to while you walk or drive. Discount stores such as Goodwill often have huge book sections offering Christian used books for $1 or $2. You can pick up several cheaply and scan them quickly for the best ideas. Reading widely in Christian fiction and non-fiction gives you a wide knowledge, perspective and information to build your faith.

A final thought in your reading: Can you stretch your reading beyond Christian books? Could you try to read the Koran (Islam's holy book) or Dianetics (Scientology book) if you found them for $1 at a store, or free at a library? Even though, as a Christian, you are not follower of these religions, scanning their books can help you directly know what other religions are about and you could speak more intelligently about them in conversation.

QUESTION 9
What kind of worship is part of your practice?

Comments: Worship refers to expressing love, respect, connection and communication to God. Dictionary.com defines the word as "adoring reverence or regard." Worship time to Christians typically means prayer, some form of music, and perhaps Bible study and contemplation time. Worship can be in a public church service or a small group or individual private time. What images come to mind when you think of the word "worship?" Maybe images of people with hands raised and eyes closed in an evangelical service, or maybe angels singing around God's throne?

Some Christians will admit they are uncomfortable with "worshipping" anything, even God. They wonder why God would want to be seemingly "idolized", as if worship means God is demanding love, in some sort of vanity or self-pride at how great he is. But perhaps worship is more like him encouraging us to connect to him, as he connects to us in many ways. Rather than being vain, he showed in Jesus that he humbles himself greatly and shows love to us.

When you go to a church service, do you feel like you worship God by focusing on him, thinking about him, or are you distracted by the immediate images and people before your eyes in the sanctuary? (We talk more about church in another section of this book). If so, perhaps your daily private time is more worshipful for you.

Oh come, let us worship and bow down; let us kneel before the Lord, our Maker. (PSALM 95:6)

QUESTION 10

How is music a part of your faith practice?

Comments: Music brings many people close to God when it stirs the soul with emotion, beautiful melodies, grand instruments and vocal choruses, and by its word concepts and stories about God. Does music touch you deeply? What formats of music are part of your practices?

There are several ways to use music in faith. One is during worship services in church: to listen, sing, hear others singing and to feel part of a group that is praising God. Are you fully enjoying songs in church? Are you concentrating on the meaning of the words and on the beauty of the music? There is much to gain there. Another way to enjoy music there is to join a choir or band at your church, even a one-time performance. It can add an extra dimension to your enjoyment of music. You hear it differently when you are in the choir. You don't have to be a good singer to carry a tune in an occasional choir experience. Can you stretch yourself to want to have this new experience?

Another way to enjoy Christian music is to listen to it outside of church on audio player, cell phone, in your car, at home, anywhere. Whether you like old hymns, choir music, contemporary Christian bands, bluegrass gospel or other types, you can listen to a favorite album or easily download your own favorite songs to make a cherished collection. Can you mention right now what songs would be on your favorites list? Listen while you are walking, doing housework or lying in bed before falling asleep. If you like Christian songs in church, but never listen to them outside of church, why is that? Perhaps a Christian radio station is an easier way for you to tune in. Set a portable radio to your local station and put a sticky note on it to remind you to tune in at a certain time of day.

A more active way to enjoy Christian music is to play an instrument, such as piano or guitar. Easy versions of hymns are simple to learn on piano or an inexpensive electronic keyboard; you don't have to be a talented player to know a few chords and notes that give a pleasing recognizable melody of your favorite hymns. It just takes a little practice. You can even progress to making up your own songs of praise as simple songs with piano or without any instrument. Think of new ways to enjoy music.

Sing for joy to God our strength; Shout joyfully to the God of Jacob. Raise a song, strike the timbrel, The sweet sounding lyre with the harp.
(PSALM 81:1-2)

QUESTION 11

What kind of service do you do to help needy people?

Comments: Jesus told his followers to help the poor, widows and orphans. We are to be servants and to show love by helping those in need, not simply to be focused on our own spiritual activities and helping our own families and friends.

Many churches are so inwardly focused that their members only think about enjoying their own church services and programs, but they never venture to serve outside their walls, opting instead for the easier way of making a financial donation to missionaries or a water well program in Africa, for example. But that is changing today. Serving with your own hands and time, meeting needy people in person, is a new idea for some Christians who want to be authentic in actually serving others. The idea is gaining popularity with conservatives and liberals alike.

To move toward action, ask yourself: Where should I serve? What would be a good fit for my likes and skills? And where and how often should I go? An easy first step is to join a church's programs of "outreach," as some are called, because they reach outside their doors. Look on churches' websites or other charity organizations for their listing of opportunities to serve. Churches do things like delivering meals to shut-ins, driving elderly people to doctor appointments, doing interior painting or yard work for disabled homeowners, tutoring students with homework or reading, make sandwiches and deliver them to the homeless in a downtown park, do a local jail visitation, or building new homes with Habitat for Humanity and so many more. Tell the volunteer coordinator you want to try out the service for a time to see if it is right for you. Consider serving with other volunteers, which will provide companionship for you.

Choose something you feel that fits your skills and schedule. Then ask yourself how often do I want to do this: weekly, monthly? What day and time? Set a regular schedule to serve. Try one service or try a few different things, it's okay to change as needed, just do something! And share your stories of service with others. Ask them to join you.

You may find that helping others also gives you great joy and satisfaction. And many people have found that the best way to get out of their own worries is to focus on helping others. Consider also the geographical component of service, by helping locally, statewide, nationally and even internationally on mission trips.

But if anyone has the world's goods and sees his brother in need, yet closes his heart against him, how does God's love abide in him? Little children, let us not love in word or talk but in deed and in truth. (JOHN 3:17-18)

QUESTION 12

How should you donate money to church and the needy?

Comments: Most people have probably heard about the Hebrew Bible's (Old Testament) admonition to give 10 percent of your income to God. However recent studies show that many Christian church members give closer to an average of 3 percent to their church. With good planning, most people should be able to give at least 10 percent to their church and other charities, but it takes a commitment and often budgeting, which many people fail to do. Where are you on the giving scale? Do you give a very small amount, or a medium or high amount? Do you have a desire and plan to give 10 percent or even higher?

The Old Testament speaks of giving of your "first fruits," meaning the first of the fruit or grain harvest, or the first of the newborn livestock. The Hebrew word for this is translated as "tithe" or "a

tenth-part." The focus here is to make your first pri-
ority to give to God, who has given you life, and
then you should have an ample 90 percent to spend
for your needs. The New Testament does not mention a specific percent be given, but Jesus comments
on some situations, such as Mark 12:41-44 where he
praised a praised a woman who put the equivalent
of a penny into the Temple treasury, which was a
lot for her, and then Jesus denounced someone else
who gave a tenth of his income with a public show
of self-righteousness (Luke 18:9-14).

The idea is to be generous and humble. Ask
yourself if you can make giving a set amount in
your monthly budgets right along with food, utili-
ties and rent. But giving can be complicated. If you
are a church member, you may have to ask yourself
if I should give my 10 percent as an overall total
to several funds of the church, such as the yearly
operating fund and a capital campaign (to build
a new building or pay an existing mortgage), and
including special requests such as for missions or
a Christmas or Easter donations. Or, some people
give five percent to their church and five percent to
some charity not-associated with their church, but
which is special to that person. They may also have
family members in need of money, and the giver
may view this as charitable giving to God within
their 10 percent. Be decisive and generous but also

careful to protect your own budget for your own safety and peace of mind. If you do not have money to give, but want to give, be creative. For example, even children have organized fund-raisers of different types that raised thousands of dollars for their church or their charity.

Be wary of religious people asking for you to give heavily to them out of a promise that God will reward you with even more money in return. God does reward us for faithfulness as a general principle, but don't treat him like a slot machine where you expect to put in a quarter and get back $100. A few final thoughts on giving: Have you examined if the money you give is being wisely used by your church or charity? Could you serve on a committee that helps raise or manage these funds (somebody has to serve, why not you?) Are you modeling giving to your children and discussing it with others who may benefit from talking about it? Why not?

QUESTION 13
How do you share your faith?

Comments: Sharing your Christian faith in its simplest terms means only telling others what you believe and do in following Christ. It does not mean trying to convince them to convert to your faith.

There has been in the past great pressures on some Christians to convert others with urgency; using hard persuasion, even condemnation, to convince non-believers they will go to hell if they do not repent and accept Jesus as savior. Many Christians felt guilty if they were not bringing new people into the faith. At the heart of this urgency was the belief by many conservative Christians that anyone who dies without accepting and following Christ in this life is headed to a fiery hell for eternity. Liberal Christians disagree by saying that a loving God does not condemn everyone to hell who has rejected him or never heard of Christ, and instead he may even give a second chance after death.

Today there is a growing desire to use a softer method of evangelism. It says to simply share what you believe, and leave that seed of information with the other person, and let God do the persuasion. You then back up that conversation with the visible modeling of a good, generous life of helping others.

But how can you bring up the topic of faith in conversation? There's always the direct option: Just ask, "What are your views on God and religion?" And then you say "Here's what I think. I think there's probably an intelligent mind behind the creation of this complex universe and complex life. I think Jesus had an incredible message and I follow him. I go to a great church that serves needy people, and I like to invite people to come check out the church if they are interested."

And after you share that message, just maybe your friend will be interested. If not, leave it to God. All you can do is plant the seed. God can take it from there. It's not up to you if someone is going decide to convert to your faith; it's between them and God. You've done your job. But, do you have the self confidence and courage to discuss your faith with someone? It's uncomfortable for many people to even try. They fear being judged, rejected, even made fun of, or they may not be sure they can defend their faith under questioning from someone else. Well, if you get a question you don't know the answer to, just say "I don't know. Let me think on that."

You may get to the point of going through the traditional steps of a Christian conversion conversation, meaning you help the other person understand that (1) mankind disobeys God's good advice on how to live (we sin, meaning turn away from God) and (2) Jesus came to earth to get our attention and help us return to God, so let's accept that and follow the many good things Jesus urged us to do, such as love and serve others. And that we need to be in a continual relationship with him to do that well. That's it. Then go out and be a witness with your actions. Maybe you will lead a blood drive at your workplace, or ask co-workers and friends to help paint a needy person's house. Wear a cross on your shirt or dress if you feel comfortable with that. Let your light shine and share your faith.

Therefore go and make disciples of all nations, baptizing them in the name of the Father and of the Son and of the Holy Spirit, and teaching them to obey everything I have commanded you.
(MATTHEW 28:19-20)

QUESTION 14

Do you display Christian art and symbols?

Comments: Christian art and symbols are a visual reminder to us and others of our faith. Symbols are seen in our homes, offices, cars, on clothes, coffee mugs and many other places. Art and symbols can include crosses, paintings, posters, bumper stickers, words on t-shirts, sculptures of religious scenes and more. Scripture passages are popular now to show as wall art. There are crosses of wood, metal and other materials. The question is "What are you comfortable with displaying? Why do you display or resist displaying art or symbols?

Some people feel displaying a Jesus message is too showy or too revealing of their private faith, or somehow is in poor taste. They say "I don't want to be viewed as a Jesus freak, or as a trendy suburban family with fish symbols on the back of my SUV." Others feel totally the opposite and see it as a way of evangelism. We've all seen the occasional car plastered with many bumper stickers proclaiming the driver's love of their school or a political candidate or showing opposition to abortion. What do you think of these?

Catholics often have religious statues in their yard landscaping. Would you ever consider doing this? As a teenager new to the faith, I had a bumper stick on my car that read "Let the Son shine in." It prompted many good conversations. Today many churches sell clothing with their logo and name on it, as well as coffee mugs and other items, which can also spark good conversations. I have a favorite oil painting in my home showing Jesus talking to the Samaritan woman at the well where he told her about living water. It is a reminder to me of that story and Jesus' message. A walk through your local Christian bookstore may show many types of art and symbols that you could purchase to display, or you could buy some online.

QUESTION
15

Do you mentor others about faith issues?

Comments: Mentoring means to give advice to someone. A mentor is defined often as "an experienced and trusted adviser" and refers typically to an older person giving advice to a younger person, but mentoring does not need to be kept only in that age structure. Mentoring is common in business, for at-risk youth and among Christians. Do you have someone to mentor in the Christian faith and do you have a mentor?

You may already mentor people on non-religious issues. You may freely give advice on relationship situations, or job or school or career topics and not realize you are mentoring. But mentoring is meant to be more than just occasional advice. It should be an intentional continual guiding someone on a path to success. If you are a parent, this is what you try to do with your children: Keep guiding them to grow and progress on the path to success.

What does Christian mentoring exactly include? It means asking your mentee routinely about how he or she is doing with their Christian practices of prayer, reading, worship, service and so on. Ask if they are making progress, becoming wiser and closer to God and of greater service. They may say they feel stuck, and you can then give suggestions. You should also share your current faith practices, telling what you are praying about and reading about, so they feel it is a sharing time also. Being a mentor is partly being a friend to walk the journey with. There may also be times you want to gently push the person: You may recommend they go for counseling, or commit to a hard course of study to take them to the next level.

Your mentoring can be informal or formal. In the informal style, you can see yourself as mentoring a friend or sibling without ever saying aloud to them that you are trying to guide them on a path to success. In a formal style, you and the mentee agree that this is a mentoring relationship and you may set a regular meeting time and have specific goals for accountability and measured growth. You may ask "Did you get your reading done this week and what did you learn from it?"

Who could be mentees for you? Younger people (including your children), people of same age, and even older people who would like a Christian friend to discuss spiritual topics with. And as you think about having a mentee, why not list that person or persons in your spiritual notebook and keep track of your progress with them.

Next, would you like to have a mentor? Think of someone you trust and would give valued advice.

Ask them if they would be your mentor and set time to talk regularly so you can be accountable to goals and growth. As a mentor or mentee you can always tell your partner that this need not be a permanent situation, let's see how it goes. That takes the pressure off. Sometimes people do not get along for a variety of reasons, but it is well worth trying to be a mentor and mentee.

QUESTION 16
Can you feel and transfer the love of God?

Comments: Many Christians seem not to be able to really connect to the phrase "the Love of God." Why did Jesus talk about love so much, saying it was the most important commandment, to love God and your neighbor? Is this the same feeling we have for a spouse, or a child or a friend or a food we intensely like?

The ancient Greeks identified four different types of love: kinship or familiarity (in Greek, storge), friendship (philia), sexual and/or romantic desire (eros), and divine love (agape). Familiarity seems like a low level of connection, while friendship is higher. A sexual/romantic desire brings in the dimension of the intense brain chemical reactions causing physical and mental attraction and even obsessive thought. God's love is described differently, as more like the intense love a parent has for his or her own child that is deeply loved: a connection, a desire to protect, to communicate often, to nurture, to see good things happen to.

But then imagine God as a creature capable of loving us a thousand times more intensely than we are able to feel as humans with our limited intellect. Imagine that he loves everyone who was ever born, and wished the best for them and helped them at times and was saddened when they abused their freedom of choice by hurting others. Can you imagine him as a being from whom love flows out like a mighty river, gushing over onto us? Can you see that love flowing out of Jesus as he embraced the broken and sick people he encountered?

Now, can you reflect that feeling of love back to God in prayer, in gratitude to him? And can you feel and even show that kind of love to everyone you meet? When you see a homeless person or a rude or mean violent person, can you look past their failures and faults and see them as someone who God loves?

Then, can you go a step further and internalize this into a habit you use every day and which can change your personality. Can you let such a love perspective make you more kind, slow to anger, quick to help, even to forgive and love an enemy?

How far could you take this? Could you pray for an enemy, and even reconcile with an enemy? If you were being crucified on a cross, could you look down and say "Forgive them father, for they know not what they do?" That sounds like a radical love meant to model something great for us to see. That was not an average human reaction. That was a person fully connected to a mighty flowing river of love and showing us something important. How can you move yourself in that direction?

Many conservative and liberal Christians disagree on what are proper ways to love. For example, many conservatives think that liberals give out love and forgiveness too quickly, without holding people accountable for their actions. An example is that liberals often favor a legal forgiveness for illegal immigrants, and liberals often oppose the death penalty for criminals. Conservatives say we can still love the illegal immigrant and the murderer, but we should also uphold strict penalties for their crimes.

QUESTION 17
Do you help with any social justice issues?

Comments: There are many injustices in the world today that need to be changed: racial discrimination, sex discrimination, and poverty, for example; things that Christians and non-Christians want to change to make society better for all. Many Christian leaders, like Rev. Martin Luther King Jr. in the 1960s, led movements to change laws to bring equality to more people. Are you interested in joining any social organizations to advocate for improvement of your country or your world, or do you leave that to persons more socially interested?

Jesus tried to right the wrongs he saw around him. A famous example is when he overturned the money changers' tables in the temple courtyard. He felt that was a practice that should be stopped. Some people feel that if Jesus were living in the world today, he would be leading non-violent protests for equality and other social improvements.

Social change often comes about slowly after long battles from two opposing sides. America had long debates and a civil war over slavery between people who thought it was acceptable and those who thought it was morally wrong, both pointing to Biblical passages to support their side. President Abraham Lincoln changed the law and finally, over time, a majority public opinion developed that slavery was morally wrong. The same disagreement process, followed by laws and consensus, occurred over women's right to vote, minorities' rights to live where they choose, and other issues. But it took people leading and supporting protests to change the laws and popular opinion. Do you wish to be part of change that is under debate and occurring now in your country?

There are many organizations working for social justice changes that you can join. A few examples are: Innocence Project works to achieve the exoneration of innocent inmates through post-conviction DNA testing; National Disability Rights Network (NDRN) works to create a society in which people with disabilities are afforded equality of opportunity; National Congress of American Indians (NCAI) works to secure the rights and benefits for Indians; National Council of La Raza (NCLR) works for civil rights and economic opportunities for Hispanic Americans; and the National Gay and Lesbian Task Force (NGLTF), the first national lesbian, gay, bisexual, and transgender (LGBT) civil rights and advocacy organization.

There are also groups working to protect wilderness, oceans, animals and many other causes. What topics are of interest to you? Could you pick one or two and join the fight to make the world a better place? Could you become more politically informed and active to elect politicians who advocate for what you think is justice?

Your views of the Bible

QUESTION
18

Do you view the Bible as a conservative, moderate or liberal on matters of inerrancy?

COMMENTS: Today in political and theological circles people are often identified as either a conservative, moderate or liberal. Conservative means you try to conserve, to limit, to preserve the current or old system. Liberal means to liberate from the current system, to change. Moderate means you may wish to do some of both, save some and change some aspects.

Christian conservatives and Christian liberals view the Bible differently. Conservatives tend to say the Bible is usually literally true and there are no errors in the book, only in the way we understand it. Liberals say that cannot be so, that there are many of Jesus' own comments that are not meant to be literally true. For example, his comment about "If your eye causes you to sin, pluck it out." Liberals say this is the use of exaggeration to make a point seriously, a common style for preachers in Jesus' day. He did not mean we should actually pull out our own eyes. Liberals take this further and say that the Bible is full of errors because it was written by men who simply thought God was talking to them or directing their thoughts, when in fact he was not, and that holding that view does not diminish their respect for the many valuable stories in the Bible.

For example, in the book of Joshua the writer says that God commanded the Israelites to kill every man, woman, child and animal in that city, and so they did. Liberals says that God, whose primary quality is love for his creatures, would not want or direct such mass killing. Conservatives says that God did direct that mass killing because it was needed to wipe out the pagan practices of those people so they would not infect the Israelite people and that perhaps death was better for the pagans than to be taken into slavery under the Jews.

Conservatives say God would not allow errors in the Bible that cause us to be confused about his will. Liberals have a different view: they believe the Bible is only a historical book written by fallible men trying to figure out who God is. God allowed errors and even wants us to challenge the scriptures.

Liberals point to the fact that Jesus challenged the Old Testament and bought new ideas to replace the old. For example, he said "You have heard that it was said to the people long ago, 'You shall not murder, and anyone who murders will be subject to judgment.' But I tell you that anyone who is angry with a brother or sister will be subject to judgment."

Many liberals feel therefore that is a model that allows us to challenge even what is written in the New Testament. Liberals says that Jesus' overall theme of love for others should override any individual passages in the Bible, because those passages, such as about homosexuality as written by Paul, do not conform with the message Jesus gave.

So how do you view the Bible, as an error free text that God inspired, or as an error filled human product that can be challenged? Or are you somewhere in between? Do you feel it would be disrespectful to God to believe the Bible is an error filled human product?

QUESTION 19

Can you explain simply what the Old Testament is about, and why it is important?

COMMENTS: The Old Testament is the Jewish Bible, and referring to it as "old" is offensive to some Jews, but to Christians it is older because it comes before the New Testament story of Jesus's life.

The Old Testament is a collection of 39 books by many authors who tell the story of the creation of the universe, animals and of humans by one creator called God, and then how God chose a people in the country of Israel to reveal himself to and interact with. He empowered a man named Moses to free the Israeli people (called Jews) out of slavery in Egypt and lead them into a fertile promised land of Israel. God gave them laws to live by and made agreements (covenants) with them, which the Jewish people broke. God turned away from helping them, and their wise people (prophets) called for them to turn back to God, saying he would restore them. God does restore them by bringing them back from exile in other lands and blesses them. This cycle of turning away and repenting is repeated.

The various books also tell how the Jewish people created over 600 laws to try to live good lives and control their people. Some were unreasonably harsh by today's standards, such as saying that a child who disobeys his parents should be hit with stones until he is killed in order to "purge evil from your midst" (Deuteronomy 21:18). Those passages are seen today by many as reflecting a practice of that violent time and the opinion of men of that time, not the desire of God. Other advice in the Old Testament is similar to the loving message of the New Testament: *"Do not seek vengeance. Don't bear a grudge, but love your neighbor as yourself, for I am Jehovah."* (LEVITICUS 19:18).

Why is the Old Testament important? Precisely because it tells the biggest stories and themes of history and we should know how they are told: the creation of the universe and of mankind, and how the creator interacts with man. And how mankind has a selfish nature that rebels against God and has been violent against our fellow people. But the message from God is to love him and love other people. Surely there is much slow reading in the Old Testament, too much historical detail of battles and kings for many people to enjoy reading, and confusing questions about whether God was really speaking through the writers or if they were speaking only for themselves in the laws and advice they created. But there is also much beautiful poetry, songs and inspiring wisdom sayings (see Proverbs). And stories about how God chose unlikely, flawed, weak people to be his best advocates and even kings in the stories that unfolded. Do not discount the Old Testament as unimportant for Christians. Review and understand its main themes, and search its pages for advice you can use today.

QUESTION 20

Can you explain simply what the New Testament is about and why it is important?

Comments: The New Testament is 27 "books," writings and letters that primarily tell the life story of Jesus of Nazareth, upon whose teachings the Christian religion is based, and the earliest activities of his followers in spreading his teachings and living by his principles. Jesus said his most important principles were to love God and to love your neighbor as yourself. He took the love concept further than previously taught in his Jewish religion by saying to love and forgive your enemies. The previous Jewish teachings emphasized an equal response when someone does you wrong, such as to pull out their eye if someone pulls out your eye.

Because the Jesus story tells of his exceeding kindness, his miracles and comments about his closeness to God, it is a basic Christian belief that Jesus was actually God coming to earth in human form to say clearly that this is how he wants people to behave. Mankind was continuing in violence and misunderstanding of God, and so God came to speak clearly his desire. As the man Jesus, he performed miracles to show his power over nature and compassion for people, and he described his kingdom and the ideal ways to live, and then allowed himself to die an unjust death as a criminal to demonstrate dramatically how a person can forgive his enemies and even to rise physically three days later to live again after death in a new type of body. It has been called the greatest story ever told, and naturally has many believers and unbelievers.

Conservatives today are most often identified as believing in Jesus as fully God and fully human, somehow blending the two into one person to achieve his goals of a message and salvation of mankind. Some liberal Christians describe themselves as followers of Jesus' teachings, but do not believe that Jesus was God or that he performed miracles. An example would be U.S. President Thomas Jefferson, who cut out all passages containing miracles and produced his own small version of the New Testament that he believed probably reflected the true life of Jesus Christ, devoid of additions that he believes were added to real stories.

The first four books of the New Testament, known as the gospels, are attributed to his followers Matthew, Mark, Luke and John. The first three books tell his life story from birth to death by mostly describing events by a historical perspective. But John's book focuses on Jesus as God coming to earth. The books following those four include 13 books by Paul of Tarsus, an enemy of the Christian followers who had a radical change and became a follower himself. Paul traveled to many cities in the region where he preached in the streets, made converts, set up new faith groups and then encouraged them by letters after he had moved on to preach in a new city. The New Testament ends with the book of Revelations, with much strange imagery about visions, but this book is believed to covey the basic message that the kingdom of God will ultimately overcome all forces that try to defeat it. The book ends with images of a garden, bringing the Bible around to where it began with a garden in the book of Genesis, and providing a satisfying conclusion amid the many mysteries.

Why is the New Testament important? Because it is the founding story of the Christian religion and the primary source of instruction for how its followers are supposed to live. The direct sayings of Jesus, such as the Sermon on the Mount, are considered of greatest importance by many, but knowing the history and advice of his followers are vital to understanding the religion overall.

QUESTION 21

Can you trust the Bible's stories are true and have been translated and copied accurately through the centuries?

Comments: Many skeptics of the Bible say that its stories were probably made up and, even if originally true, were probably changed so much over time as they were translated between languages and copied by hand many times that they have lost all reliability.

Conservative Christians argue today that different types of evidence point to the even the earliest stories as being based on real events. For example, archaeological discoveries in the 1920s confirmed the presence of cities much like Ur, described in Genesis 11. Engravings discovered in an Egyptian tomb depict the installation of a viceroy in a manner that exactly matches the biblical description of the ceremony involving Joseph (Genesis 41:39–42). And regarding translation accuracy, believers point out that when the Dead Sea Scrolls were discovered in Israel the 1940s near the Dead Sea, they were 800 years older than any other available manuscripts, and yet comparing them to later copies of the same books showed a high degree of consistency for those Old Testament books. Even these few examples, some people say, shows that the Bible overall can probably be trusted as true and accurate, and they further believe God would not want or allow his holy book to contain errors.

Liberal Christians argue a different viewpoint about all Bible stories as true and accurately copied. They say that some of the stories are probably based in true histories, as shown by archeological finds, but others may not be, especially considering that early people commonly exaggerated or changed stories told orally as they passed through the generations and early eras when accuracy was not as valued or verifiable as today. Other stories were meant to be symbolic and not literally true, as perhaps Jonah swallowed by a big fish. So, liberals say, they take a "maybe approach" to stories and passages' trueness. Maybe they are true, maybe they are not true, we cannot know for sure and we should comfortably accept that uncertainty, while focusing more on the importance of the overarching messages of Bible history and the advice of Jesus on how to live.

For example in the virgin birth story, they say, the word "virgin" was more probably accurately translated as a "young woman" in the original language used, and was wrongly translated. Even some letters of the apostle Paul are thought by scholars to be frauds written after his time by people who attached his name for various reasons. This belief comes from the wide differences in theology and vocabulary compared with others of Paul's letters. Scholars often judge authenticity by comparing ideas, words and phrases the author used in his well-trusted works, and comparing to see if those are consistent in the questioned works.

Regardless of where the Bible may have errors, the life of Jesus was verified by external sources, such as the early historian Josephus, and therefore the belief in him as a real person with a unique message is widely accepted.

QUESTION 22

How can you interpret (understand) the Bible?

Comments: When people talk about interpreting the Bible, they generally mean how can they understand what is meant by a particular part or passage. In anything we read, including non-religious materials like letters or poetry or song lyrics or books, the author may mean something different than what we immediately think he or she means. Haven't you ever listened to song lyrics and wondered "What does that mean?" There may be double meanings or only part of the story told, and you fill in the rest with your thoughts. The message may be aimed at people just for one time or place, or for people everywhere and all times, for example. A love song, for example, may describe one person but can be felt by the listener to apply to their life too.

Here are a few tips that Bible scholars give to understanding the Bible. They involve asking yourself a few questions.

Ask: What is the "context" of the passage? Context means the "full setting" of the words or quote, including the comments that come before and after a specific statement. Politicians and others often rightly complain they are "taken out of context" when a few of their words are lifted from a longer comment, such as saying "I would vote for a tax increase, only if it was needed to save lives" and then only the first few words are reported.

Also try to understand Bible passages in relation to what is in the rest of the chapter and in the rest of the Bible regarding that topic. That is wide context. For example, ask "Does this one passage agree with other similar sayings on this topic, or does if differ greatly?" Christians and Muslims can pull out individual passages about violence from their holy books and base their actions on a few passages they like, but what do their whole books say and what did the authors' mean?

Ask: Who wrote or spoke the passage and to whom was it addressed? Does the beginning of that Bible book or chapter say who wrote it or said those words? Was the author an eyewitness to events and seemingly reputable or educated and seemingly unbiased? Were the words addressed to a specific person or specific church for a specific situation (like some of the letters of Paul) or were they addressed to a crowd (like the Sermon on the Mount) to seem more like general advice for all people?

Ask: What does the passage say exactly? Maybe there are concepts or certain words you should investigate further, using a Bible commentary or a web search.

Ask: What is the historical and social setting when the passage was written? Was this written by a person raised in the midst of an especially violent or primitive time who may have been so strongly affected by that setting that it colored everything that he or she wrote to the extent that you may question the application of that advice in today's world?

Methodists also have a four part guideline to understanding the Bible that was created by Methodism's founder, Rev. John Wesley. Wesley said to rightly understand the Bible, one should use scripture, tradition, reason and experience. Wesley insisted that scripture is the first authority. But, opinions and practices from the history of the church, our traditions, are also important. We should also use our own human reasoning that God gave us, he said, but we should ask to be helped by the Holy Spirit. And finally, our own human experience helps us to become wiser and understand Biblical issues.

QUESTION 23

Do you memorize and recite Bible verses?

Comments: Being able to recite Bible verses from memory can be a great aid to you and others. But some Christians are afraid if they go around quoting verses they will sound too religious or will appear to be showing off. Or they think that memorizing verses sounds too hard. But you probably already have several memorized, such as the famous John 3:16 (For God so loved the world that he gave his one and only Son, that whoever believes in him shall not perish but have eternal life.) Or you probably know the Lord's Prayer (Our father who art in Heaven, hallowed be thy name....).

How can reciting verses to yourself help you? It can bolster you faith and emotions in trying times, improve your memory and reinforce your understanding of spiritual issues. And reciting passages to other people can help them do the same.

How can you memorize? Pick favorites. Try memorizing one passage a week. Then each week review the one from the week before along with a new one. Repeat the passages every day. Think on them, how they apply to your life. Share them with friends. Soon, talking about your favorite passages may become a common thing in your conversation and will remind you and others that you value the Bible and do not hesitate to talk about it.

Here are five famous verses:

ROMANS 8:28: *And we know that in all things God works for the good of those who love him, who have been called according to his purpose.*

PHILIPPIANS 4:13: *I can do everything through him who gives me strength.*

PROVERBS 3:6: *In all your ways acknowledge him, and he will make your paths straight.*

ROMANS 12:2: *Do not conform any longer to the pattern of this world, but be transformed by the renewing of your mind. Then you will be able to test and approve what God's will is—his good, pleasing and perfect will.*

PHILIPPIANS 4:6: *Do not be anxious about anything, but in everything, by prayer and petition, with thanksgiving, present your requests to God.*

SECTION FOUR:
Some of the Big Questions

*What do you believe
about the Trinity?*

Comments: A traditional Christian belief today is that God is one person in three forms: the Father, the son Jesus Christ, and Holy Spirit. They are of one spirit, perhaps of one mind, but in three forms, similar to the concept of water that can be in liquid, frozen and steam forms.

But where did this idea come from? It is not explicitly stated in the Bible that God is three equal beings. It appears to be put together by followers in later years, as they believe they came to understand what was in the Bible. For example the gospel of John describes Jesus as existing with God from the beginning. And then Jesus said the Holy

Spirit comes from God as a comforter. But do these clues mean Jesus and the spirit are also fully God?

Historians say that the early Christian Ignatius of Antioch gave support for the Trinity around the year 110, exhorting obedience to "Christ, and to the Father, and to the Spirit". The first of the early church fathers to be recorded using the word "Trinity" was Theophilus of Antioch writing in the late 2nd century. He defines the Trinity as God, His Word (Logos) and His Wisdom (Sophia).

Conservative Christians today are often identified as those who fully accept the concept of the co-equal three-form God, while liberals are identified as those more likely to challenge the concept. Some liberals says they prefer the concept of God the father creator as one separate person, and the other two as having a spirit and wisdom and power similar to his, much as a human father and his children would share the similar personalities and attributes. But some conservatives counter by saying that to resist the Trinity idea is simply our human minds having to always separate things to understand them. For example, we think of humans as always male or female, however there are people and other organisms on the sex scale that blend aspects of male and female; they do not have a clear identity as one or the other. God could blend identities among three forms if he wants to.

Considering the positions of the believers and skeptics, what are we left to do with the concept of the trinity? Perhaps we should say it is certainly possible for three to be as one, and that we hope to find out the details when we get to Heaven?

QUESTION 25
What do you believe about the afterlife, Heaven and Hell?

Comments: Where did the concept of a life after death come from? Some say it first came is a natural human impulse of earliest man to believe that our thinking mind consciousness, our soul, goes to another place when the body dies. Maybe it seemed logical to earliest man that it came from somewhere and goes to somewhere. Some say there are clear Old Testament references to an afterlife with God, such as Isaiah 26:19: *"But your dead will live; their bodies will rise..."*

But not until Jesus spoke of the afterlife are there such clear descriptions and promises. Jesus spoke of himself going to where God lives and preparing a place for us to join him in a place with many rooms. Then he showed by his bodily resurrection that there clearly was life after death for him, and by his promises also life there for us. John 13:19 quotes him as saying "Because I live, you will live too." And John 3:16's promise that eternal life is for people who believe in Jesus.

Many questions arise about the afterlife. Here are few. What are Heaven and Hell like? Do we go straight there after death, or is there a death sleep until a judgement day? Is Heaven only for those believers who repent and confess Jesus as their savior and follow him? Do the near-death experiences of people indicate they really went to Heaven and came back, or were those hallucinations caused by chemicals in the brain?

Can you read those questions and give your opinion quickly? Do you care? It can seem easy to answer these questions from a conservative or liberal standpoint. We may say that conservative belief generally has been that Heaven is a place of golden streets and gardens where we all live with our family and friends who have gone before, and that only people who repent and accept Jesus in this life will go to Heaven. The rest go to a place of burning hell fire for eternal torture, as indicated by some stories in the Bible.

Liberal Christians today say that a loving God would not send good people to a burning hell of torture simply for not accepting Jesus in this life. They believe a second chance to accept God is probably available after death, and that even if people are in a Hell they can still turn to God (as Christian writer C.S. Lewis speculated that Hell is "locked from the inside," indicating people can get out by their own choice). Liberals say the Hell fire stories were meant to be exaggerated fictional stories told in the style common in the old era and intended to convey the idea of fear in being separated from God, not literal stories of live souls in an actual burning place of afterlife. The stories are rooted in the word Biblical word "gehenna," meaning a valley south of Jerusalem that was a burning trash dump where bodies and human sacrifices were thrown, and which was continually burning, they say.

Many books about Heaven, Hell and the historical scholarship of their questions are available today if you are interested. While some followers of Christ today do not believe in either a Heaven or a Hell, some also believe in only a Heaven, and they regret that few preachers today talk about the glorious hope of a wonderful afterlife with God and family in a place of no more sickness or tears, as the Bible promises. Preaching on that seems to have gone out of style, they say, as skepticism even among Christians is rising. Yet the story of Christ's resurrection and other Biblical passages give a wonderful, although limited view, of a Heaven that is worthy of looking forward to, even as we focus strongly on doing God's service on earth.

QUESTION
26   *Why does God allow suffering?*

Comments: This is perhaps the biggest question of all the God questions. Why would a God who loves us allow such terrible suffering to occur in this world, even suffering of innocent children? People say "If I were God, there would be no suffering." And since there is suffering, they think maybe that is a strong clue that there really is no God, and the Bible stories of a loving God are completely made up.

But as Christians we believe that God is like us in some ways (he loves) and yet different from us in many ways (he is spirit, he is eternal, he is all-knowing). The Bible also says his ways and thoughts are different than ours. Isaiah 55:8 "For my thoughts are not your thoughts, neither are your ways my ways."

So we may ask, is it logical for us to expect an eternal spirit to act like we would in the matter of temporary sufferings? Could there be a higher reason he does not intervene to stop suffering? Consider times when a human parent allows their child to suffer through a circumstance, from a baby's normal crying to even a teen's time in jail, to produce a greater result or personal growth. The Bible says in James 1:2 "Consider it all joy, my brethren, when you encounter various trials, knowing that the testing of your faith produces endurance."

So we know that tough times can produce wisdom, patience, and stronger character. But it still nags at us that there is a high level of suffering in this world, as though there is no God to step in to stop extreme and unjust suffering. And when we say the answer is a mystery, it seems a cop out, too easy to push the mystery button and accept that explanation. But is it so wrong to accept that we cannot know that answer and try to be comfortable with it while still keeping a faith in God. Can we accept that this is one of many things that our three pounds of human brain can not understand? Does this one hard question have to destroy our faith, as it has for some people? Perhaps we disagree with God on this one, and still love him. We can still believe that God is with us in our suffering, as he was with Jesus during his suffering, and that his perspective is higher than ours.

QUESTION 27

Do the smartest people believe in a creator God?

Comments: Among some Christians there's the occasional thought that perhaps the smartest people in the world have the right answers about God, because they know how to evaluate information and come to the best conclusions that humans are able to find. But is that true? Do the smartest people come to the unbiased, truest answers?

Scientists, for example, are often seen as the smartest people. They think deeply and try to figure out the complicated physical laws of the universe. So what do they believe? Albert Einstein, among the greatest, did not believe in a personal God of the Bible, but wrote "The problem involved is too vast for our limited minds... The child dimly suspects a mysterious order in the arrangement of the books but doesn't know what it is. That, it seems to me, is the attitude of even the most intelligent human being toward God." So he seemed agnostic, unsure if a creative intelligent single mind was behind the creation of the universe. Einstein's final opinions were shared in a letter he wrote one year before his death, in 1954. Einstein wrote to the philosopher Erik Gutkind that "The word God is for me nothing more than the expression and product of human weakness, the Bible a collection of honorable, but still purely primitive, legends which are nevertheless pretty childish. No interpretation, no matter how subtle, can change this for me." (Source www.inquisitr.com/).

On the other hand, a modern scientist who believes in a personal God is Francis Sellers Collins (born April 14, 1950), an American physician-geneticist noted for his discoveries of disease genes and his leadership of the Human Genome Project. He is director of the National Institutes of Health (NIH) in Bethesda, Maryland. Collins has written books on science, medicine, and religion, including "The Language of God: A Scientist Presents Evidence for Belief."

Of course, many high IQ professional scientists, doctors, lawyers and others are on both sides of the belief spectrum. In forming opinions, highly intelligent people are subject to the same biases as less intelligent people, such as the biases imparted to them by their teachers and family and peers who are for or against a belief in God, and the smartest people also face a desire to be accepted by their peers on matters such as religion and politics, perhaps resulting in the trend today of atheism as being fashionable among academics.

Studies have tried to analyze the religious beliefs of smart people. A 1921 study by Lewis Terman, a psychologist at Stanford University, involved recruiting 1,500 children whose IQ exceeded 135 at the age of 10. This data was re-examined by Robin Sears at Columbia University in 1995 and by Michael McCullough at the University of Miami in 2005.

The conclusion of both these reviewers was that the children were less religious when compared to the general public. However, what was remarkable about the data collected by Terman was that in spite of their atheism, 60 percent of the children he studied were brought up in 'very strict' religious homes. (Source www.dailymail.co.uk). Perhaps these youth were rebelling against the religion of their strict family, an often normal reaction?

Another explanation is that intelligent people do not like to accept any beliefs that cannot be tested, according to an article in Arstechnica.com.

Many people today seem swayed by a trend of thought in recent times that mankind is discovering so much more about the world that we no longer need the "myth" of a God that created the world. Matter and physical laws themselves could be eternal and there is no need for an intelligent mind to have created them, some scientists say, and are trying to prove that. They say that as we once thought seizures were caused by demon possession, now we know it is a physical condition, and so our knowledge will increase until we no longer need to believe in a creating God, they say.

But perhaps God hides himself from the smart and the average person, delighting as we search for him and debate about him, which keeps us talking about him. After all, we know that God does things differently than humans, and perhaps he smiles as the intelligent person dismisses the simplistic stories of the Bible. But could those simple, even seemingly foolish, stories point to a truth about the real existence of a personal creating God? 1 Corinthian 1:27 says "But God chose the foolish things of the world to shame the wise; God chose the weak things of the world to shame the strong."

QUESTION 28
Can you name the basic beliefs of the major religions?

Comments: Do you have religious ignorance? Ignorance means not knowing. Some Christians know very little about their own religion and nothing about other religions, even though they may work with or be related to people of other religions. But having some knowledge of other major religions gives you information to compare your own beliefs against others, and to talk with some knowledge and interest to people of other faiths. So, let's review a few elements of what four major religions believe.

Christians believe in a loving God who created all that exists and revealed himself by coming to earth as a man named Jesus about 2,000 years ago. With the dual identity of human and divine, Jesus told the people of his day that God did not primarily want religious rituals from them, but rather for them to love and help each other and to have a close relationship with God. To show he was God, Jesus performed miracles, forgave people of their sins and said that anyone who believed in him would have an eternal life. Jesus rose bodily from the dead and promised that his followers would do the same. Christianity's holiest book is called the New Testament and tells the story of Jesus' life and teachings.

Judiasm, the religion of the Jewish people, focuses on relationships between man and the one creator God, and between people. The Jewish holy books, called the Old Testament by Christians, tell the story of God creating the universe and humans, and later revealing himself to the man Moses and giving him 10 laws for people to live by. There is no formal set of beliefs that a person must hold to be a Jew, but there are 13 "Principles of Faith" that were compiled by Rabbi Moshe ben Maimon, a medieval Jewish scholar. These include: that God exists, God is one and unique, God is incorporeal, God is eternal, prayer is to be directed to God alone, the words of the prophets are true, Moses' prophecies are true, and Moses was the greatest of the prophets, the Written Torah (first 5 books of the Bible) and Oral Torah (teachings now contained in the Talmud and other writings) were given to Moses, there will be no other Torah, God knows the thoughts and deeds of men, God will reward the good and punish the wicked, the Messiah will come, the dead will be resurrected.

Muslims believe there is the one God, named Allah, the creator of the universe and the source of all good and all evil. Everything that happens is Allah's will. He is a strict judge, who will be merciful toward followers depending on their good works and religious devotion. Muslim honors several prophets but Muhammad is considered the last prophet and his words in the holy book the Koran are the authority. Muslim's have to follow five religious duties: 1. Repeat a creed about Allah and Muhammad; 2. Recite certain prayers in Arabic five times a day; 3. Give to the needy; 4. One month each year, called Ramadan, fast from food, drink, sex and smoking from sunrise to sunset; 5. Pilgrimage once in one's lifetime to worship at a shrine in Mecca. At death -- based on one's faithfulness to these duties -- a Muslim hopes to enter Paradise. If not, they will be eternally punished in hell.

Buddhists do not worship any gods or God. The Buddha (a man named Siddhartha Gautama) never claimed to be divine, but rather he is viewed by Buddhists as having attained what they are also striving to attain, which is spiritual enlightenment and freedom from the continuous cycle of life and death. Most Buddhists believe a person has countless rebirths, which inevitably include suffering. A Buddhist seeks to end these rebirths. Buddhists believe it is a person's cravings that cause these rebirths. Therefore, the goal of a Buddhist is to purify one's heart and to let go of all yearnings toward sensual desires and the attachment to oneself. Buddhists follow a list of religious principles and very dedicated meditation. When a Buddhist meditates it is not the same as praying or focusing on a god, it is more of a self-discipline. Through practiced meditation a person may reach Nirvana -- "the blowing out" of the flame of desire.

QUESTION 29
Do you do "religious travel"?

COMMENTS: Traveling to Christian holy sites and cities with deep religious history can have a great impact on your faith and practices. Do you have a desire to go to Israel, Rome, Greece or other places where the earliest Christian events occurred?

In Israel you can actually walk in the places that Jesus walked, such as the Garden of Gethsemane, which has been preserved in its exact location and appearance with Olive trees over the centuries.

You can be baptized in the Jordan River, very near where historians believe Jesus was baptized. Doing this gives you vivid mental pictures for the rest of your life so that when you read the Bible you visualize exactly the places the events occurred. In Bethlehem you can walk into the cave where Jesus was very likely born. In old Jerusalem, you can walk the route that Jesus walked from his trial before Pilate to the small hill where he was crucified (Calvary), where you walk up several steps to an altar and look down upon the rocks where he likely spent his final hours on the cross.

In Rome, Italy you can see the Mamertine Prison where the apostle Paul spent his last days and wrote two of his letters. At St. Peter's Square you can stand near where St. Peter is believed to have been crucified upside down, and then go in St. Peter's Basilica church where he is believed to be buried underneath in an original burial cave. In Greece you can visit where Apostle Paul traveled on his missionary journey through Philippi, Thessalonica, Athens, Corinth and other places as you retrace the steps of the most influential missionary of Christianity.

But many people do not want to travel to holy sites. There are many obstacles for them. Among the top reasons are a feeling that Israel is dangerous and that traveling takes too much money, time and physical effort. The truth is that terrorist violence rarely touches tourists in Israel. Arabs and Jews both benefit economically from the constant flow of tourist groups to their Arab and Jewish areas and so neither group wants to disrupt that. The violence is usually aimed directly and narrowly at the enemy, not a tourist areas, hotels or buses. The obstacle of money for a religious travel vacation has varied solutions: some groups or churches may offer to pay for your trip based on need and income level, or you may be able to take out a loan, or save the old fashioned way to pay cash for a trip.

For people who are firmly never interested in going to religious sites, there is a next-best option if they still want to see the places: watch a documentary video. Many of these travel tour videos are so good, you will feel almost as if you have been there. You will understand the sights and their historical significance. To find them, search the Internet for "religious travel videos."

Another form of religious travel is service trips, also called mission trips. Going to help paint a church in a small town, or build a simple home in Mexico for a few days, or clean up a city ravaged by a tornado can be a rewarding religious experience for an individual or a family. In fact, it can be more rewarding than religious travel for many people because it is outward focused, it helps others, and is not inward focused on your own education.

QUESTION 30 — *Why does God stay invisible?*

Comment: Some people say "If I were God, I'd show myself to humans, or at least give undeniable evidence that I exist." Perhaps they would like for him to appear in the sky each day at sunset and speak to us in a booming voice. Or perhaps he could walk among us every Sunday morning, healing everyone in need. What would a world like that look like? But since God is spirit, and his thoughts are higher than ours, as the Bible says, perhaps there are perfectly good reasons that he remains hidden from our view. Perhaps our small brains could not comprehend him if he appeared fully as he is. And, of course, the New Testament says he did appear to man 2,000 years ago in the form of Jesus of Nazareth, doing miracles and explaining how man is meant to live. Does he need to appear on a certain timetable, say every 2,000 years to update his story to convince skeptics?

It is certainly true that it is difficult to live your life dedicated to someone you cannot see or hear in conversation in a human way. It's not hard to understand why many people say they will not believe in something they cannot perceive with their physical senses: sight, hearing, touch, taste, smell. But are there not many invisible things that people believe in: love, wind, hope? And aren't there scientific theories that people believe in without having overwhelming evidence? Why should belief in an invisible creator of the universe be such an unlikely theory?

God told Moses in Exodus 33 that on Earth "no man can see my face and live." But in Revelations 22 the author says of Heaven that "...the throne of God and of the Lamb will be in it, and His bond-servants will serve Him; they will see His face, and His name will be on their foreheads, and there will no longer be any night; and they will not have need of the light of a lamp nor the light of the sun, because the Lord God will illumine them;.."

Many Christians look forward to a day when they see the face of God, even to talk with him in a human style conversation of back and forth. But until that day, can we be patient with an unseen creator? Perhaps his invisibility keeps us searching, questioning, debating. Can we accept and be comfortable with that?

QUESTION 31

What are a few main arguments to believe in God and the ways people try to refute them?

Comments: There are many types of arguments, including cosmological (about the cosmos, the universe) and psychological (using mental reasoning to think about God). One of the most persuasive arguments of wide appeal to many people is the Intelligent Design argument. It goes like this: The universe and living creatures are staggeringly complex in themselves and the way they relate to other things. The universe and life also appear so designed in their complexity that it seems to us that only an intelligent mind could have created this order. The chances of this complexity occurring without a creator are so small that is exceedingly unlikely, some experts say. On the other hand, skeptics say that given enough time in a universe where planets are continually being created and dying, it is possible that such complex life could eventually develop and it does not necessarily mean an intelligent mind created it.

Another argument is that everything that is created must have a creator, and God is that creator. But, then as children sometimes ask, "Who created God?" The answer is that God is the only uncreated thing and has existed forever. Skeptics disagree and say the laws of physics and other dimensions could be the one eternal thing and that our universe popped into existence from other dimensions without an intelligent mind causing it.

Psychological arguments for God include the reasoning of people who believe that life after death experiences of seeing a Heavenly place and a person of light are real. There is also the "argument from common consent" which asserts that religious belief in a creator has been widespread throughout human history. It seems to be an inborn belief that is common to many people, and therefore it is an instinct toward something that really exists. Humanity seems to have a common agreement (consent) that there is some kind of creator, which we call God.

Is there one or more reasons, or arguments, that seem true to you? Which ones and why? If you are interested in reading more about religious arguments for God, do an Internet search for arguments for God.

QUESTION 32
What is religious doubt and how do you deal with it?

Comments: How certain are you that your beliefs are the objective truth about God? Can you put a percentage to it? Are you 100 percent totally certain

God exists? Some people who have had visions or near death experiences may say they are totally certain, for they believe they have seen Jesus welcoming them. The apostle "Doubting Thomas" may have said he was 100 percent sure of Jesus after he put his hands into the nail holes of Jesus resurrected body. The rest of us have occasional doubts.

Doubts are only natural for our situation as humans connecting with a non-human spirit, whose "thoughts are higher than ours," as scripture says, and whom does not interact with us in the normal human ways of being visible and speaking aloud to us. God communicates differently to us, through the Bible and our own thoughts and probably by mysterious coincidences that cannot be explained. No wonder we doubt. But if we learn to accept and live with doubt in this life, it can spur us to think and question and seek spiritual matters more often than if we had no doubts at all. We trust that God has a reason for not being visible today in human ways, and for leaving us in doubt. We can believe and have some degree of doubt at the same time, as contradictory as that sounds, but we do it all the time with many beliefs. I may believe it is going to rain today after seeing storm clouds and hearing a local weather forecast say there is a 90% chance of rain, but I have some doubt. Can you name other situations where belief and doubt live together?

SECTION FIVE:
About Your Local Church

Why go to church services and get involved in a church?

Comments: Church services are gatherings of usually like-minded believers who want to learn about and worship God together. Among the benefits of attending a church worship service are to learn and be inspired by a sermon, to pray with others, to enjoy worship music together, and learn about many programs the church has for doing things of the Christian life.

Sure, a local church is also like a social club for Christians. The members often socialize together and get important emotional support from that. But a good church is much more than a club. It is also a place that organizes service projects for the needy, holds classes to learn about and discuss the Bible, provides support groups for those in need for support, and provides a holy sanctuary where you can come to worship and feel close to God.

Yet, for many people, even some Christians, going to a church building is not what they want to do. They may feel that they'd be unwelcome, or unworthy, or were previously offended by preachers they have seen or heard in person or on television. A church atmosphere is not appealing to them, so they stay home and read the Bible occasionally, by themselves, never connecting to others, missing out on the many benefits a good church can provide. Do you know someone like that? Would they come to visit your church and be warmly welcomed there?

Today there are also many alternative types of churches, meaning other ways that the traditional church building with a steeple. There are church services in bars on weeknights where attendees have a beer while hearing a short sermon and music. There are "home churches" in which groups meet only in living rooms in small groups. There are Internet-only churches where attendees sit in front of their computer to watch a service. Perhaps one of these are more suited for you than a traditional church? The point is to think about connecting with other Christians and growing in your Christian life.

The Bible says that we should not forsake "our own assembling together, as is the habit of some, but encouraging one another; and all the more, as you see the day drawing near," (Hebrews 10:25)

QUESTION 34
How to choose a local church, or why did you choose your church?

Comments: If you are looking for a church to visit or join now, what should you look for? Or, if you are in a church now, why did you pick that one, and are you still comfortable there? Consider these six factors:

Beliefs: What religious beliefs does the church promote? Many promote basic Christian beliefs, but with their own emphasis on a conservative or liberal interpretation, which may be clearly stated on their website, especially with regard to controversial issues such as acceptance of homosexuals at their church. Ask a regular member what the beliefs are. And if you are a regular member, what would you say if a visitor asked you what your church believes?

Size: number of members is important for many people. Would you like a small church of a few hundred people or fewer, a medium size of maybe 1,000, or a mega-church of more than 2,000? Small churches have a homey feel where everyone can get to know each other. Large churches can feel overwhelming, but can provide a small feeling by getting in small groups.

Worship service format and style: Do you like the format of the worship service, meaning the order and length of the events? Some churches have long prayer times, long music and a long sermon. Others have short sections. What are you comfortable with? Visit in person or watch a service of this church on the Internet.

Senior Pastor's preaching style and topics: a key factor is whether you like the senior pastor's preaching topics and his style (assuming the senior pastor gives most of the sermons). Does he or she yell at you or lecture at you? Do you learn and get inspired or moved to think deeper on a topic? Does he or she actually teach from the Bible and talk about God and Jesus, or are they rarely mentioned? Watch or listen to several of this pastor's sermons on the church's website.

Location and facilities: Is the church close to your home or an acceptable distance from you? Do you like the design, décor and feeling of the church building? Think of that as you walk around the building.

Programs: What does the church offer in terms of child care, music, Bible classes, small groups, men's and women's group events, service programs to help the needy and other programs? Does it have programs that you would like to join? See their catalog of programs and events.

There are many other factors to consider also, but these are some of the basics. Perhaps no church will perfectly fulfill all your criteria, just as when you are looking for a house to buy, but you may know quickly when you have found a church that makes you feel at home and where you can be served and you can provide service.

QUESTION 35
Are you a "one hour Sunday Christian?" at church?

Comments: When you go to church on a Sunday morning or maybe even a Saturday night service, is it for one hour only? Perhaps that's how you view the "Keep the Sabbath" commandment, by giving up one hour of your Sunday to hear a sermon and music. Many churches try to get you involved in more than one hour: they encourage you to attend a Sunday morning small group discussion or Bible Study class, or to teach or assist for one hour in a children's Sunday School class. The point is: can you do two hours and enjoy a bit more with God and for God?

Maybe you're doing good to be there for just one hour. That's okay. But perhaps you should think about how to be there for one more hour and all the benefits that you and others could derive from it. Also think about the hours in the Sunday afternoon or evening. Could you devote one hour there to reading a bit deeper in the Bible, praying a longer prayer, spending time with a needy friend to serve them? That is a way to be more than a one-hour Sunday Christian. If you had to estimate, how many hours a week do you spend in Christian study, service, prayer or thought? It's just an idea to see how important the Christian life is to you.

QUESTION 36

Are you connecting with your pastor and church members?

Comments: If you go to church, are you connecting on some level with the pastors and the church members beyond the typical "Hello. Nice to see you?" Are you their acquaintance, meaning you've met them, or are you friends, meaning that you occasionally spend some time together, or are you a close friend, meaning you spend recurring regular time together and have frequent communication?

Take the senior pastor, for instance. Many people do not develop a close relationship with their pastor because he or she is seen as the busy author-ity figure. The congregants do not think to really befriend him or her, have meals with him, or to see if he wants to be your friend. Perhaps you and the pastor have much in common and he or she wants a new friend to confide in and meet regularly, even for lunch once a month. Have you considered that? There is no right or wrong answer. It depends on what both of you want, if your personalities are compatible, and so on.

The same goes for your relationship with other church members, especially new members. Do you see someone there you can try to be friends with? If you try and are rejected, at least you tried. Simply move on. You can set limits on how often to get together or communicate. You usually have to take the initiative, make the first move to invite them to meet. Jesus' command is to love our neighbors. This is one way to do it.

QUESTION 37

Are you a member and active participant in your church?

Comments: Have you joined your church as a mem-ber or are you a perpetual visitor? Are you always thinking you may join in the future or maybe you are not interested in joining at all?

For many Christian churches, to join simply means that you are asked to give your prayers, your regular attendance, your gifts of financial help and your help of service. And there's the problem for many people. They don't want to be committed, to be tracked, to get letters from the church asking them to give money or come help in a service project. They just want to show up on Sunday morning when they feel like it and have nothing asked of them and give nothing but an occasional $5 bill dropped in the collection place.

But the Christian life is meant to be more. God asks his people in the Old Testament to enter into covenants with him, to be faithful to him and follow his way of life. The New Testament encourages people to gather together, to support and pray for each other.

Yes, joining a local church is a bit like getting married. It is an expression of commitment. It says I like this place and these people, I will support them and will participate to the degree it is possible for me. And as a member who regularly gives an amount of money you have determined, it helps your church to plan for its budget and ministry work when the leaders can estimate how much money is promised to come in. Do you want other people to give money regularly and then you just show up and receive the benefits of their giving?

Perhaps for a while it needs to be that way for you, but hopefully not your whole life.

Once you are a member, you may feel more connected to the church and people. Perhaps your photo and contact information will show up in the church directory of members. And membership also allows you to serve in leadership roles by being a member of committees of the church, such as a Council, which sets policies, a finance or building or personnel committee. Have you considered serving on one of these now or in the future, or do you leave that to others you feel are more qualified or interested? What if no-one decided to serve on those committees? Of course there are many other ways to be an active participant in your church. To be in small groups, music groups, service groups. How do you plan on being an active participant rather than a passive participant?

Where Do You Stand On Social Issues?

QUESTION
38

Do you view social issues through the Bible?

Comments: Social issues like abortion or immigration refer to actions that affect society in important ways, issues that we have to make laws about to control our society and avoid harm to people. But it is often very hard to agree on what is harmful. One person may see all marijuana smoking as harmful while another sees it as beneficial for medical conditions or recreation. So how do you decide where you stand (and vote) on a complicated issue?

As a caring and thoughtful Christian, you want your faith and the Bible to be the lenses through which you shape your views. Let us ask, what does the Bible say about this topic directly or indirectly?

And if there are passages that seem to contradict each other on this topic, how do I resolve that? Let's look at two current social issues from a Christian perspective and the question of how to choose between political candidates.

QUESTION 39
Is homosexuality wrong in God's view?

Comments: For many people, this question may stem from whether they believe the Bible is a collection of God's direct infallible messages to mankind, or whether the Bible is a collection of man's often-faulty efforts to understand God.

If, as many conservatives believe, every bit of the Bible is God's word to us, then the passages in the Old and New Testaments saying homosexuality is wrong are true statements of God's timeless intention on the topic. On the other hand, liberals believe that many of the Bible writers were simply wrong about what they think God intended, and God let them be wrong in their writings because we have free will, so the writers reflected their own biases and understandings of the time they lived in. At the time, they thought slavery was acceptable, to value women less than men was acceptable, and all homosexuality was wrong.

Liberals say that we have come to see that slavery is wrong and that equality for women is right, despite individual passages in the Bible that seem to say otherwise, so we should do the same for homosexual rights because it is consistent with Jesus' main message of treating all people with love and respect.

Conservatives counter by saying that there is also a natural order of design, in which we can clearly see God made male and female with natural affections for the opposite sex. Liberals reply that, yes that is true, but just because a small percent of the human population has a genetic variation that causes them to be attracted to the same sex does not mean God wants them to live their whole life without a partner, and love and affection.

And so the debate continues back and forth. Conservatives say there's no need to make it so complicated because the Bible is clear on the subject. Liberals says it's not clear because Jesus did not speak directly about homosexuality, and Paul's references on this topic in the New Testament were meant in their original language to condemn homosexual relations with children, not to a loving consensual relationship among adults as it is understood today. So how does a Christian today make a decision on this topic? Perhaps by considering both sides, doing your own research and thinking, and praying for God to lead you in a decision.

QUESTION

40

What is a fair policy about illegal and legal immigrants?

Comments: Love your neighbor and the needy, welcome them into your home. Serve them. Those are some of the Christian commands. But what happens when immigrants flood into a country, overwhelming schools and hospitals with their numbers? Is it unloving or just tough love to deny any more of them entry?

Some conservatives say America should send back all illegal immigrants and their children. That would seem not very welcoming. But they broke the law, correct? Isn't that fair? What about someone who stole a loaf of bread to keep from starving? Should they be jailed, or forgiven due to their desperation?

Again, Christians should make decisions based on Jesus's commands to love and forgive all people, and on Bible passages, using our own experience, tradition and reason. What is reasonable and balanced to welcome people and to protect your own country and people? Often a compromise is best. For refugees and illegal immigrants, you can recognize their desperation, and therefore forgive and welcome them, make them pay a fine and taxes perhaps, and contribute to America, while simultaneously stopping the flow of more immigrants to an amount your country can handle.

Some see the key as whether you are acting and speaking with love, even while you stand firm, or are you simply trying to look tough by rejecting immigrants, with no regard to Christian values. In forming social views, look to reflect Christ, reflect balance as he did between love and firm opinions, take all factors into consideration, and take a stand. Don't avoid taking an opinion as you get stuck in fear of rejection perhaps by your peers, or stuck in the paralysis of analysis of much information. Form an opinion, even share it with your legislator, even act on it to help an immigrant or others if you can, and then move on.

QUESTION 41

How should Christians choose between political candidates?

Comments: Christians should want to be informed and active voters to help ensure that we have good leaders who will make reasonable laws at all levels of government: local, state and national. But too often we ignore this civic responsibility because it seems too boring or too complex to be worth our time. Let others do that, we think. Are you registered to vote?

Christians should support candidates who have qualities and goals that Jesus and the Bible commands: to love people, forgive, help the poor, do justice and speak with kindness, be humble and honest, to name a few. The U.S. Presidential campaign of 2016 brought this into sharp view for many people with a choice between Republican Donald Trump and Democrat Hillary Clinton. Trump's harsh and demeaning words against some women, Latinos and his opponents revealed his deep lack of true compassion, kindness and humility, critics said. Clinton's changing stories on issues such as her use of personal email accounts for government business showed her problems with honesty and good judgement, critics said. For many voters, the choice was a lesser of two poor candidates. But it often is. You will agree with candidates on some of their issues and actions, and disagree with them on others. The question should be: Overall, which candidate is a person with the best combination of good character, skills, experience, knowledge and judgement for that office to make reasonable decisions that moves our city or country forward to help people?

Christians do not always support the overtly Christian candidate who makes frequent mentions of their faith or an appeal to religious voters, and that is probably a good thing. Look at the candidate overall. The U.S. Constitution states that "No religious test shall ever be required as a qualification to any office or public trust under the United States." Americans are more open than ever to electing people of any faith, or no faith, as long as they are the best candidate to make good decisions. America was founded as a place for freedom to practice any religion you choose, without persecution; as a place where people of many faiths and races should be able to live together in harmony, working for the good of all people, not seeking to further their own religion at the expense of others. This is an unusual idea in a world where people in many places still seek to impose their religion or views on others by force and government law. America and other democracies seek to be tolerant of varied people who are trying to live in harmony. It is a testament to tolerance and trust when Christians could vote for a Muslim or an atheist who seems the best candidate.

If you are not registered at your county election office, register online and choose to have an advance mail ballot sent to you. When the ballot arrives, spend a few minutes researching the candidates you do not know by looking at their websites that state their positions on issues and the qualifications. Mark your ballot and mail it back (or vote online if possible), and then share with other citizens that you think voting is important.

Where To Get News and Entertainment

QUESTION 42 — *Why should Christians care about where to get news and entertainment?*

Comments: Thinking Christians today want to be well-informed about news and social issues so they can live out our mission of making a better world for all people and enable all people to hear the messages of Jesus Christ. Part of being well-informed and open minded is to get both sides of the stories that are reported: the pro and con.

Many cable TV news or radio talk shows today promote only one side: either the Republican or the Democratic, the conservative or liberal agenda. They may even say they are objective or balanced, but you can see that they give much more information from one perspective. Even the seemingly neutral outlets, such as the main TV network news shows and major newspapers, can tilt their coverage toward one side. When you read or hear news of an issue or person, ask "What is other side of this story? What is the positive and negative about this issue?"

Intentionally seek out secular and Christian news and entertainment from many sources. For news, do you view TV, radio, newspapers, magazines and websites? For video entertainment there are so many secular and Christian TV shows and movie options today. Let me recommend a few.

QUESTION 43
What are good sources for Christian and secular news?

Comments: Many Christians today seem to avoid Christian-focused news sources and TV shows, perhaps because they see these outlets as being too preachy or one sided. But here are some good news outlets of balanced presentation. Give them a look. You might like to visit them on a regular basis by marking them as "favorites" on your website lists.

CHRISTIAN-FOCUSED NEWS

NEWSPAPERS: Here are three newspapers and their related websites that offer religious news content. (1) *The Christian Post*. This website (http://www.christianpost.com/) has perhaps the widest variety of Christian focus stories (news, arts, columns) than any other about the Christian religion around the world. You may not agree with its columnists opinions, but the news stories will inform you. (2) *The Huffington Post*'s religion section (go to "all sections" tab, then "Voices" tab, then "religion tab") is a section of this California newspaper that offers thoughtful columns and news from a variety of voices, when many big newspaper have no religion section at all. (3) *The National Catholic Reporter* website is also packed with news and theology columns. Even if you are not Catholic, this is still Christian news and views and reflects events in our world. The stories are written to pull you in, such as one recent with the headline "16 common theological errors that Catholics should avoid."

MAGAZINES: Here are three magazines. (1) *Christianity Today:* written from a conservative viewpoint, it is available both online and in printed format and covers world, national, church and ministry news. (2) *RELEVANT* Magazine is a bimonthly lifestyle magazine with a focus toward faith, life, and culture. It targets 20-something's who are passionate about God, spirituality, and the world they live in, the website says. (3) *Bible Study* Magazine is a new, growing print magazine for Christians who want to dig into the Word of God, its website said. This publication is offered six times a year, delivering tools and methods for Bible study, as well as insights from Bible teachers, professors, historians and archaeologists.

TELEVISION: (1) *Religion and Ethics Weekly* (PBS channel), tells news and features on all religions from a very objective viewpoint. Check your guide for when this weekly show airs, or for video replays on its website. (2) *Christian World News* on CBN network shows news from around the globe, and you can watch latest episodes on its website at http://www1.cbn.com/cbnnews/shows/cwn. (3) *Religious cable TV channels* such as Church channel or Daystar or EWTN (the catholic channel) have varied programming, from book reviews of books by Catholic authors, to swarthy protestant TV preachers yelling and begging for money. It is interesting to surf the channels occasionally and see what religious shows are offered in today's culture.

Radio: Religious radio news and talk shows most often come in the conservative format. Religious music shows on radio come in traditional and contemporary formats. Many have devoted listeners who get great help and comfort from these shows. Do an Internet search or just flip your radio dial to look for some in your market. See what they offer.

Secular news: Meaning non-religious. Where do you get your regular news and information from? Do you pick it up from TV only? From comments on social media? Here's a suggested way to be better informed in just a few minutes. Every week, visit a source to get news from four levels: your city, your state, your country and your world. You probably have a city newspaper with website. Then also go to the city newspaper of your state capitol, to get more state news. Then see a national newspaper or website, such as the New York Times, to get a national perspective. And then go to an international source like the London Times, to see what is going on abroad and how it is reported. The variety should be interesting to you. Be a news traveler.

Final tips on how to use the news: Visit varied news sites once a week. Read first for headlines to find topics that interest you, then read the story. Think who you can share this story with that would benefit from it. Think how to use this information in your life and ministry to others. Send a gift subscription to one of these publications to a Christian friend for a birthday, Christmas or just to share.

QUESTION 44

What are good entertainment sources for Christian and secular movies and TV?

Comments: There are good fiction and non-fiction movies with Christian themes that should appeal to you, inspire your thoughts and your faith. Why not seek them out occasionally? Think of these in categories, such as old classics, newer films, TV movies and documentaries. Find them on your TV on-demand service or borrow from your library, or order DVDs from the Internet.

Old classics: A few favorites are The Ten Commandments (Charlton Heston), King of Kings (Jeffrey Hunter), Ben-Hur (Charlton Heston), The Robe (Richard Burton, Jean Simmons), Martin Luther (a 1950's black and white).

Newer films include: Luther (Joseph Fiennes, Sir Peter Ustinov), The Mission (Robert De Nero, Jeremy Irons, Liam Neeson), The Passion of the Christ (Mel Gibson directed), Chronicles of Narnia: The Lion, the Witch and the Wardrobe, The Nativity Story (Keisha Castle-Hughes).

TV movies: The Red Tent, Abraham (TNT: Richard Harris, Barbara Hershey), Jacob (TNT: Matthew Modine, Lara Flynn Boyle); David (TNT: Leonard Nimoy, Nathaniel Parker)

Documentaries: Amazing Grace: 5 Hymns That Changed the World, Obstacle to Comfort: Life of George Müller, Bonhoeffer: Pastor, Pacifist, Nazi Resister.

Secular TV and movies. How should you think about non-religious shows as a Christian? Some say putting garbage into your mind affects your thinking and your faith, and includes excessive exposure to violence, profanity, explicit sex, and extreme dysfunctional people continually arguing and acting selfishly. It may be entertaining to watch like a car wreck, but is it good for you? Pornographic movies and videos, for example, are an extreme and can clearly become a destructive obsession. Perhaps awareness of using your good judgement is a key. Don't let yourself get sucked into watching TV or movies repeatedly expose you to terrible behaviors. Build up yourself and your faith life with good images and examples of good entertainment.

SECTION EIGHT:
Your View of the Future

*What is the future of
your Christian life?*

Comments: Do you want to keep steadily growing in all the aspects of your Christian life, or are you satisfied to stay at the level you are now? Each of us could continue to become a bit more effective as a servant helping the poor, wiser in our understanding of theology, better at prayer, and so on. Wouldn't that be a good goal for our Christian lives?

One way to go about that is to write down such goals in your prayer notebook or simply be aware and strive for improvement regularly. Compare yourself to where you were 10 or 30 years ago. Are you more of a servant, and wiser now? You could set a few easy goals on how to improve. If you are helping the poor just once a year now with your hands, try for once a month now. If you are not reading the Bible regularly, put it on your calendar to do for even 10 minutes on Wednesdays and Saturdays, or get in a study group. If you are not memorizing scripture, try two new scriptures on note cards and repeat them back while you are driving.

The point is to think about your future faith. Perhaps our faith journey starts when we come into relationship with Jesus Christ and continues forever forward, always growing. Or do you think that you are satisfied with where you are now on Earth. Some Christians feel they've read it all and asked all the questions and see that there are still so many mysteries that we might as well wait until we are in Heaven where we may have perfect knowledge given to us. But perhaps in Heaven you simply keep growing in knowledge at a steady rate, as you are able to on Earth.

QUESTION 46

What is the future of your family's faith?

Comments: Do you envision your family as a Christian group with members at different places on their faith journeys? Do you envision each of them growing in faith and service in the coming years: The children, the young adults, the middle adults, your own spouse, the grandparents? You could take an interest in each of them, talking to them about their Christian beliefs and practices, and encourage them to view their own future as a journey of growing effectiveness in all areas of faith. Of course, this falls under the mentoring category, even in the mildest form of only talking with someone occasionally on the topic to encourage them.

Maybe your family is a dynamic part of one local church, and you foresee your children in the future as being leaders in that church. Or perhaps your family, like many, is a mixture of people of different faiths and no faith. What if one of your children were to join a very different faith or marry someone of a different faith? Could you accept that easily? Doing a mental survey of the faith of your family members, and your possible roles of influence, can be helpful.

QUESTION 47
What is the future of your local church?

Comments: If you are a member of a local church, do you ever wonder what it will look like in 20 or 50 years? Many churches shrink in attendance to the point they are simply closed and the few remaining members go somewhere else. But if your church is a vibrant place that is teaching, serving the community and living out the Christian mission, don't you want it to continue for a very long time? Could your clergy and lay leaders do long term planning and thinking to help that? Why not try to do a tentative 20 year plan? Imagine what will the neighborhoods around the church look like, will they be redeveloped, will young or older families likely live there? City planners do such projections, you could get input from them.

How might American culture be different in 20 years and how will your church's style and message appeal to people then? One frequent comment today is that the next generation will have no concerns about welcoming gay people into all areas of church life, including having gay pastors and doing gay weddings. Will your church be one of those, or offer a conservative alternative to that?

Will your church offer something different or timeless, to draw a particular niche in the church of the future? Can you lay groundwork now for church programs, youth activities, social activism and service that will keep people interested and connected to the church for 20 or 50 years? Some senior pastors set a vision and tell the congregation of the 20 and 50 year plans, inviting people to think way ahead. Maybe that includes plans to have satellite church branches, or to move the main church building into a new area. Why not dream and share the vision?

QUESTION 48
What is the future of Christianity as a world religion?

Comments: We hear about research saying that the number of Christians and churches are shrinking in Europe and America. But their numbers are growing in Africa and Asia. And the number of Muslims, followers of the Islamic religion, are growing much more rapidly. Some people worry that Islam will dominate the world, and its followers persecute Christians worldwide as more Muslims move into positions of leadership to make laws. Others say that even if Islam dominates in terms of numbers, it will be a moderate form of peaceful Muslims who will want to co-exist with people of all other religions.

We also hear some people predict that all religious belief will eventually fade as humans come to see that science finds all the answers to life's questions, and there is no need to believe in an invisible God. We will discover that matter and physical laws have eternally existed and that our universe popped into existence naturally from another universe or dimension, without any help from an intelligent mind creator.

But there have always been predictions that religion will fail, and yet there seems to be an inborn desire to seek out the divine, to connect to the creator. Christianity's amazing story of Jesus' message and life will continue to have great appeal because it makes sense to many people. Love and forgiveness and peace and service are the best ways to live, and will hopefully gain growing acceptance as mankind develops in wisdom over time.

One thing that seems certain at this time is that the word "religion" today has negative connotations, conjuring images of hateful, intolerant Christians in bloated church systems. Many young people say they are "spiritual but not religious." They want an experience of faith but are wary of institutions. They want to serve and to have meaning. How will the church of the future address that?

QUESTION 49

Does the future contain a Christian rapture, tribulation and second coming of Jesus?

Comment: Many conservative Christians debate the "end times" references in the Bible regarding a "rapture," the taking away of Christians into Heaven, and a 1,000 year period of misery called "tribulation" and a "second coming of Jesus to Earth." Many are convinced these will happen someday and have debated the meaning and order of these events predicted in the Bible. Many liberal Christians, on the other hand, dismiss these things as probably visions or predictions of the future that were not really inspired by God, but rather the thoughts of the authors or things added later to the Bible by translators.

However, they are hard to dismiss when Matthew chapter 24 records Jesus saying that his followers will see him "coming on the clouds of heaven with great power and glory" and that "this generation will not pass away until all these things have happened." But what does this mean? His followers at that time reportedly thought it meant he was coming back in their lifetime, in their generation, so they were ready for his return. But since he has not returned on the clouds since he left, some people today say perhaps Jesus said that as a way to keep his believers thinking of him and being vigilant in living as he commanded, but this imagery was not meant to be taken literally.

Two thousand years later many Christians are still waiting for his return with a trumpet blast in the sky. Revelation describes an important time of 1,000 years when Christ rules. Some sources say that his concept was first proposed by the ancient Persian religion of Zoroastrianism.

Whatever the truth, there is little we can do to know the details, so this is one more area where we accept the mystery of the Bible. Perhaps Jesus will return with a trumpet blast, so let us live as though he will return today. Perhaps he will not return to Earth and this was a symbolic story to encourage keeping your faith strong. Perhaps a final war called Armageddon will occur, or perhaps it was the prediction of well-meaning ancient prophets who thought their vision was from God. Let us accept that we probably cannot know while on this Earth, and be comfortable with leaving it in God's hands.

QUESTION 50
Where do we go from here?

Comments: So now that we have asked ourselves all these questions, how should our Christian lives go forward from here? My hope is that by reviewing these questions, and especially the varied faith practices, we have a greater awareness of the many ways to live the Christian life. But you may ask "Who can reasonably do all those many faith practices all the time?" A reasonable answer is that you don't have to do all of them every day. Spread them out on your calendar. Do a service project once a week or month. Pray a written prayer once a week. Read the Bible every other day. Maybe read another spiritual book every other week.

But keep a list of what you plan to do. Pay attention to enjoying and growing in your Christian life. See your human life journey through the lens of yourself as a spiritual being on a journey leading to God. See your faith and your religious practices as the most important thing at the very center of what is you, not as just one more thing on the outer circles, as you may a hobby. See your identity as a Christian as your primary identity, the most important, followed perhaps by your family role, career role and others. If you do that, it will ground you and make you want to do those many faith practices. Be decisive. Don't be stuck in the paralysis of analysis, thinking someday I will do something on that certain area of faith practice. Put it on your calendar and stick to it. So go forth, make yourself into a disciple: a passionate, committed, visible follower of Jesus and a teacher of his Way. God bless you.

About The Author

STEVE BASKA is a former newspaper reporter and editor who leads an adult Sunday School class in his Methodist church and has taught in the Disciple class series of Biblical studies. He and his wife, Vickie, live in the Denver area. For more information, go to www.stevebaska.com.